Wisdom and Virtue

Wisdom and Virtue

The Tao Te Ching Decoded and Paraphrased

Kevin M. Thomas

WISDOM AND VIRTUE
The Tao Te Ching Decoded and Paraphrased

KETNA Publishing
P.O. Box 90861 Burton, Michigan, 48509

Copyright © 2018 by Kevin M. Thomas

All rights reserved. No part of this book may be reproduced or transmitted in any form or by any means, electronic or mechanical, including photocopying, recording, or by any storage or retrieval system without permission in writing from copyright author.

For more information, address to KETNA Publishing
P.O. Box 90861, Burton, Michigan, 48509

First KETNA Printing Edition 2018

Cover Design By: 99designs
Interior Design By: Medlar Publishing Solutions Pvt Ltd., India
Proofreading By: Kelly Bixler and Sean Burns
at www.thewriteproofreader.com

is a registered trademark of KETNA Publishing
Printed in the USA

Library of Congress Control Number: 2017917733
ISBN: 978-0-9963874-3-9 (soft cover)
ISBN: 978-0-9963874-4-6 (hard cover)
ISBN: 978-0-9963874-5-3 (ebook)

Dedication

This book is dedicated to those who want to understand the powerful simplicity of the Tao Te Ching. It is also dedicated to my parental rocks, June and Grover, who made their own personal transformations over time. To my children, Isiah, Caroline, Kimberly, and Cheyenne, my unconditional love for you will always remain in my heart. And last but not least, I dedicate this book to God, who helps me stay on His great path. Without Him, I am nothing.

Acknowledgments

To God, your love guides me on the great path that You put me on.

To my dad, Grover, who became the best earthly father a man could want, now looking down and watching my path from above.

To my mom, June, you always took care of me and said the right thing when I needed it most. How fitting it is that I now have the privilege of doing the same for you.

To my children, Isiah, Caroline, Kimberly, and Cheyenne, may your lives be guided by unconditional love and forgiveness, for these are the things that make life worth living.

To all those who have really supported me, including family and friends, I thank you.

Table of Contents

Introduction . . . .*xi*

Chapter One 1
Chapter Two 2
Chapter Three 3
Chapter Four 4
Chapter Five 5
Chapter Six 6
Chapter Seven 7
Chapter Eight 8
Chapter Nine 9
Chapter Ten 10
Chapter Eleven 11
Chapter Twelve 12
Chapter Thirteen 13
Chapter Fourteen 14
Chapter Fifteen 15
Chapter Sixteen 16
Chapter Seventeen 17
Chapter Eighteen 18

Chapter Nineteen 19
Chapter Twenty. 20
Chapter Twenty-One. 21
Chapter Twenty-Two. 22
Chapter Twenty-Three. 23
Chapter Twenty-Four 24
Chapter Twenty-Five. 25
Chapter Twenty-Six. 26
Chapter Twenty-Seven. 27
Chapter Twenty-Eight. 28
Chapter Twenty-Nine 29
Chapter Thirty 30
Chapter Thirty-One 31
Chapter Thirty-Two 32
Chapter Thirty-Three 33
Chapter Thirty-Four 34
Chapter Thirty-Five. 35
Chapter Thirty-Six 36
Chapter Thirty-Seven 37
Chapter Thirty-Eight. 38
Chapter Thirty-Nine 39
Chapter Forty 40
Chapter Forty-One 41

Chapter Forty-Two 42
Chapter Forty-Three 43
Chapter Forty-Four. 44
Chapter Forty-Five 45
Chapter Forty-Six 46
Chapter Forty-Seven 47
Chapter Forty-Eight 48
Chapter Forty-Nine. 49
Chapter Fifty. 50
Chapter Fifty-One. 51
Chapter Fifty-Two. 52
Chapter Fifty-Three. 53
Chapter Fifty-Four 54
Chapter Fifty-Five. 55
Chapter Fifty-Six. 56
Chapter Fifty-Seven. 57
Chapter Fifty-Eight. 58
Chapter Fifty-Nine 59
Chapter Sixty 60
Chapter Sixty-One 61
Chapter Sixty-Two 62
Chapter Sixty-Three 63
Chapter Sixty-Four 64

Chapter Sixty-Five. 65
Chapter Sixty-Six 66
Chapter Sixty-Seven 67
Chapter Sixty-Eight. 68
Chapter Sixty-Nine. 69
Chapter Seventy 70
Chapter Seventy-One 71
Chapter Seventy-Two 72
Chapter Seventy-Three 73
Chapter Seventy-Four 74
Chapter Seventy-Five 75
Chapter Seventy-Six 76
Chapter Seventy-Seven 77
Chapter Seventy-Eight 78
Chapter Seventy-Nine. 79
Chapter Eighty 80
Chapter Eighty-One 81

About the Author *82*
Wisdom and Virtue. *83*

Introduction

The *Tao Te Ching* is the most translated book in the world, next to the Bible, and has grown in stature through the centuries to help make up a solid foundation for Taoism itself and Chinese Philosophy, and is central to Chinese religion. In addition, it is also a main source of creativity and inspiration for the Chinese people and others around the world.

In a nutshell, it was originally made up of eighty-one brief chapters or sections from over five thousand Chinese characters, and the text was additionally broken into two parts: the Tao Ching, which makes up chapters 1–37, and the Te Ching, which is chapters 38–81.

The *Tao Te Ching*, which can be translated to mean the "path of virtue," was written about 600 BCE, according to the Chinese by Laozi, also known as Lao Tzu or "Old Master." However, the authenticity, dates, and authorship are still debated, as some claim that even two authors were involved.

Another problem is that the complexity of the Chinese characters, when translated to various English versions, left more riddles than answers and made a tough reading for those looking for a quick application of the wisdom within. In fact, most of the English translations are mystical and obscure at best. Because these versions were difficult to read and unusable to modern westerners and others who were hungry to apply its principles for a better life, there was a need for this book to be decoded and paraphrased.

Additionally, one will also notice from these summarized verses within that there is a correlation between Christian text and perhaps a proverb-type reading. In fact, Christian missionaries made a connection between Taoism and Christianity, and between the *Tao Te Ching* and the New Testament. Could Eastern and Western religion be more linked than we originally thought?

Through the years, the *Tao Te Ching* has become the path or the way for those seeking wisdom on this journey we call life. Finally, my wish for you is that you enjoy this paraphrased and decoded version created for those seeking an easier understanding and application, and that your path always be blessed.

Chapter One

The great path is not just the heavenly path, but also the earthly path that leads to heaven and contains the wise advice used to reach this goal. God is the beginning of heaven and earth, and so the question must be asked: What is our plan on Earth to ultimately be able to see the unseen God? For if we don't follow the right path, evil and consequences will result. So the main question becomes, will you follow good or follow evil? Finally, we must also ask, what does God want for us? These are all important questions on the journey.

Chapter Two

All things are not as they appear to be, so we should remember the adage, "Be careful not to judge a book by its cover." Following the path requires many things—for example, a blending of hardness and softness for the path to work. Sometimes, we must be gentle, and sometimes, we must be more assertive. But in the end, there is no desire for ourselves (wu-wei), but for a spiritual path, according to God. We can't change it, but we can only do our best with humbleness to follow the path God wants for us.

Chapter Three

Be fair and be humble; don't praise some people and forget others. Don't put some people on a pedestal and put down others, for when this happens, it brings forth jealousy and conflict. Next, don't brag about what you have, for it will only cause other people to crave it. There is no need to show off. To lead people, you must get people to trust you by getting them to relax, by treating them well, by feeding them, by letting them measure up, and by strengthening them. When you accomplish this, you will not have to worry about people scheming against you.

Chapter Four

The great path involves a wealth of knowledge and is encompassed by many things. Overall, this path is made up of love, compassion, and togetherness. So in the end, it is overflowing in these very things, and ultimately, is the core of the great path.

Chapter Five

God does not regard people lightly or with disrespect. He knows your thoughts and dreams and fears. In fact, heaven and the earthly path you follow blend together along this journey. And be sure, it is a journey to be experienced fully rather than a journey to just talk about. So open your arms and embrace this path.

Chapter Six

Mother Earth is also known as the "valley spirit" and is a form of Mother Nature ruled by God to control events on Earth. This is the root of natural events that God uses to achieve His purpose.

Chapter Seven

We have the assurance that in some form, heaven, Earth, and God last forever. They are never-ending, and they live forever.

Chapter Eight

The great path must be absorbed and embraced, but it can be difficult for some people because they hate what is good and love their evil thoughts and desires. So while on Earth, think on what is good, live with gentleness and self-control, and approach these evil-doers with compassion, presenting the path to them without coercion so they will change their ways. And if you do this, you won't be responsible for their fate.

Chapter Nine

Have pure motives. Don't be a person who always wants their way and is caught up with greed and material things. Don't be one who is puffed up with bragging and boasting, for if this happens, eventually, you will lose what you have.

Chapter Ten

Let go of material things, and focus on the oneness of the path. Live with balance in love and law when following God, and while considering someone else's point of view. Be able to give to others without expecting something back, do your best, and never be a know-it-all. And finally, be like the child who is happy by just being in the moment.

Chapter Eleven

When we follow the great life path, we must be careful about what we put in our minds. Certainly, we should keep an open mind and be receptive to others, but we should not clutter our minds with useless things that take us off course. Instead, always move forward with focus, and keep your eye on the great path.

Chapter Twelve

The primary goal of your life should be to get to heaven, and this can be done with a simple life. In fact, seeing too much, experiences of the wrong kind, and gathering too much takes you off the right path. Therefore, take the path that leads to an eternal life in heaven, for even though the physical body dies, the spirit lives forever.

Chapter Thirteen

One way to stay on the path is to be humble and to live without personal desire and with a pure desire to please God. This will keep you grounded and free from being ambushed with the criticism that often comes regardless of whether you have fame or fortune or whether you are poor. So practice humbleness, be at peace with yourself, and be a servant for all. For in the end, if you can help the world with your service, the world shall respond.

Chapter Fourteen

What is the great path? Well, it cannot be seen or heard or touched, but when looking for it, when listening for it, when reaching for it, it fills the senses, and all these things become one. It is shapeless, colorless, and will exist from the beginning to the very end. The great path has not changed over centuries and is both the spirit and the essence of the journey to heaven.

Chapter Fifteen

Past teachers experienced the spirit and path in a profound way because they used great wisdom. They were able to master those traits to make the journey successful. They moved carefully and used caution and did not get sidetracked with things that could take them off course. And yet they were joyful and open to others, and they continually took unclear teaching and made it clear to all without the desire for personal gain. So let us all learn from these wise teachers.

Chapter Sixteen

Isn't it wonderful to know that there is value in just being, that we can have very little, but do much for others? And if you plant just a seed in others, it will grow. Additionally, the path brings many actions, including a time for quiet thought and reflection. And at other times, it requires sharing and being more engaged and active. The path is also impartial, and if you act on your own wishes instead of those of the path, harm may come. So be open and receptive of the path, for it is the way to the kingdom of heaven, which is the eternal way that lasts forever.

Chapter Seventeen

From the beginning of time, the great path has been known; some loved it, some praised it, some embraced it, and some even hated it. So for each person you meet, be sincere and careful with your words, and try to work well with others. Not everyone will be on your side, but if you spread the credit to everyone for accomplishing a goal and don't take all the glory for yourself, all can happily share in the reward.

Chapter Eighteen

Be careful when you walk along the great path because you will encounter false teachers who will attempt to destroy or distract you with their foolish intellect. They also want to destroy the path itself and your spirit. They also claim to know the way, but it almost always leads to chaos and a loss of compassion. Ignore their pleas, and stay close to the right path.

Chapter Nineteen

Be true and pure of heart. Get rid of false piety and morality, all while claiming higher wisdom. This is the wrong path. Instead, have character even when no one is around. For when you falsely claim that you are giving but are actually hording riches, you yourself will be the victim of robbery. So truly reflect on what you need to do so you will not become greedy with desire.

Chapter Twenty

The great path is not just learned from a book, but must be experienced with lessons and knowledge applied. So don't spend too much time dwelling on unanswered earthly questions. The journey requires great sacrifice, so consider this: I am everywhere, but without a home, and others appear happy, but with false joy. I may feel alone and tired while others enjoy earthly treasures, but I know that I must leave material possessions behind to follow the great path. Still others seem noticed and appear happy, while I am ignored. Yes, it seems I have no place to rest while others pursue earthly pleasure. I may not understand this totally and know that I am different, but I also know that I am carried by the very root of the path for my benefit.

Chapter Twenty-One

Faith and belief are the cornerstones of this great journey. And while the great path can be followed, it cannot be described. It is simply indescribable with its vastness of knowledge, but it is always there for your benefit if you are wise and follow its ways.

Chapter Twenty-Two

Following the path is not complicated; in fact, it provides all the answers for those who use a simplistic approach. Once you recognize this and are open to its truth, the truth will be revealed to you; and if you continue on the great path, you become an example for all others. So always remember that the path is already complete and perfect; it does not need to force its way or brag or desire, and it is not contentious. Just believe in its completeness and follow it.

Chapter Twenty-Three

God has already decided on the direction of heaven and Earth, so don't try to change the world and create continuity. Instead, focus on the great path until you and the path become one. However, be warned: you will be presented with two paths, and either path may appear to be the happy way to go, but only one path is the right way. And when you are on this path, you will earn the trust of others.

Chapter Twenty-Four

When on the great path, keep a low profile and don't confront people or brag about what you have or what you have done. Instead, stay humble, for it is useless to go any other way that only feeds the ego and is disliked by all. And remember to always stay balanced, and never stray from the right way. But if you do stray, return to the right path as soon as you can.

Chapter Twenty-Five

The great spiritual path existed before heaven and Earth were fully formed, and it will always exist as the great path until the end of time. The path is so great, it transcends both time and place. Among the great things God created, there are four things that are among the greatest, and they are: people, Earth, heaven, and the great spiritual path. This is because humans depend on the Earth, the Earth is dependent on heaven, heaven depends on the great spiritual path, and all depend on God.

Chapter Twenty-Six

Always focus on what needs to be done, move forward, and bare your heavy burdens. Don't be distracted by the things of this world. Otherwise, you will lose the very foundation you and your family have achieved, as well as the ability to show others the great path.

Chapter Twenty-Seven

Those on the right path must teach those that are not. This begins with valuing and loving people instead of creating stress with fault-finding. When you accept people with love, you can elevate them by lighting their path, and they will come to accept you and what you show them.

Chapter Twenty-Eight

Be balanced in life—a mixture of both gentle and strong. And when you approach people, be open and non-judgmental, and serve as an example for others. Remember, when you stay on the path, your path will be abundant. So listen and become one with the great path and your life will become whole and complete.

Chapter Twenty-Nine

Don't look to rule the world, otherwise you will fail because of your greedy manipulating. Therefore, stay away from excess, overestimating your ability, trying to be something you are not, and thus becoming overbearing. Remember, sometimes in life, not everything will go our way when following the right path. Oh sure, sometimes things go right, but sometimes they go wrong, and that is just the way it is. However, no matter how things look today, we must stay on the great path. For overcoming the obstacles will allow for the greatness of the true way to be revealed.

Chapter Thirty

The beauty of the path is that it ensures a fair give-and-take along the way. And without the path, you are more likely to go to war with people and dig your own grave. So if you intend to argue with others, stop this action. Also, it is good to achieve some things in life, and the path allows you to do this with humbleness and without bragging. So don't force your way onto others and brag about what you have accomplished; this would be the wrong path.

Chapter Thirty-One

Using weapons is an unfavorable thing to do. No real, honest soul likes them, and the man on the wise path does not use them. So whenever possible, make your position one of peace and not war. If you have to use weapons, do so as a last resort and with no joy. For only those who like to kill are happy to use weapons, but nobody trusts them. This is because regular citizens have to shed tears when they bury their own, which causes further mistrust of leaders who go to war or of those wanting to cause harm.

Chapter Thirty-Two

When following the great path, don't worry about having a title, because the path doesn't need certain credentials to follow it. The road will not always be easy, and some will be unable to cope, which can cause divisions among you. However, if you have no fear and aren't misled, many things will fall into place, and then the balance of Earth and heaven will open up to guide your way. Wisdom is knowing to stay on the path to keep you from falling.

Chapter Thirty-Three

If you understand others, you are intelligent. If you understand yourself, you are wise. To overcome both yourself and others to do what is right is power. To not be envious of others is to be truly rich. And if you live with great energy and passion when following the right path and hold nothing back, you will live forever.

Chapter Thirty-Four

The great spiritual path cannot be stopped. Though it can require much effort to survive on the journey forward, it will only be slowed temporarily. So if an obstacle appears and you get sidetracked, return to the path on your own accord and without manipulation, and the path will reveal its greatness.

Chapter Thirty-Five

Cling to the great path, and you will always have peace. Those distracted by wine, food, and other pleasures will eventually be harmed. However, those on the great path have useful gifts, and it will present itself in how you feel, your spirit, and the oneness with the great way that can lift you forever. And always remember, it's there for the taking if you are wise.

Chapter Thirty-Six

Coming to the path, in essence, means starting over and a rebirth of spirit. This happens by emptying out the old ways and then rebuilding with what is new. And by resisting your past, you begin on a new journey of enlightenment. When you do this, it will then shed further light and reveal that peace and gentleness are more effective tools than aggressiveness and fighting, which often leads to failure. In the end, one path leads to prosperity, and one path leads to harm, so choose wisely.

Chapter Thirty-Seven

The great path encompasses all things, but its beauty is in its being as opposed to just doing. Its power comes from the faith of believing rather than just accomplishing tasks. So wise leaders should embrace what comes naturally and be receptive to what the path offers, for when this happens, heaven will be pleased.

Chapter Thirty-Eight

Who you are on the inside is important on the great path, for being moral on the surface is not real morality. Putting on airs and pretending to be nice is deceptive, for true goodness and morality is not manipulative or done for selfish reasons. So if you pretend to have a person's best interests at heart and don't, they will become angry with you. If you appear to be loyal and sincere and aren't, it will anger people even more. So being real through our entire being, no matter how deep someone looks, is important. Then we can honestly look at how a situation really is, rather than how it appears to be by knowing the person and knowing the facts.

Chapter Thirty-Nine

Wholeness is being united as one with the great path, for God's path is clear. While life on Earth can be rough, the peace and spirit of the path will fill the void. This will then lead to a prosperous and compassionate life; and if you are a ruler, it will make you more effective, for competent rulers do not create divisions, nor is this God's true desire. Remember this: without the path, Earth would not be strong and peaceful, good things would vanish, and rulers would be ineffective. So make your journey a humble one, with the lack of desire for material things, and then watch the greatness of the great path reveal itself.

Chapter Forty

When you come back home—back to the great path—your burden will be lighter. And at the same time, you will be honoring your personal existence by going from a cast-off or non-person to a spiritual being full of wisdom.

Chapter Forty-One

Superior students hear the great path and follow it. Some students in the middle hear it and sometimes follow it, but sometimes fail to do so. Then there is a third group of students who don't understand it and just laugh it off. Why? Perhaps it's because the great path is long and tedious and not easy. It also requires sacrifice and sometimes requires going against the crowd and standing alone. It can also take a long time to master the path because it can be mysterious and difficult to grasp in a changing world. But as we explore the world, to reach our true higher self, we must become superior students.

Chapter Forty-Two

The great path designed by God yields itself in a yin and yang harmonious way. For instance, some may lose what they don't need or have—a desire that is not good for them. Some people may actually gain something, like a needed material possession or wisdom. So following the right path with discernment is important, for it is prosperous and leads to heaven, while the wrong path leads to demanding one's own way with impulsive force, which would just lead to the demise of oneself.

Chapter Forty-Three

The great spirit moves for your benefit. One of the most important aspects of following the great path is reacting to the world in both a positive way and without personal gain. This may not always be easy, but one of the best ways to accomplish this is to remember that gentleness and our spirit overcome strife and the world.

Chapter Forty-Four

Along the journey, a person may need things to carry them on in terms of possessions: clothes, tools, food, and even some money. However, the useless or greedy desire for material possessions and overaccumulating worldly goods that you don't need can come back to haunt you and take you off the right path. Therefore, having balance in life and knowing when to say "enough is enough" is an important lesson to learn.

Chapter Forty-Five

We can attempt to walk the right path and try to be perfect along the way, but unless we truly grasp the bigger picture of peace and reveal a clear view of ourselves and the path to others, then what we do is useless. The true path may seem like a grand way to go for some and look contradictory to others, but overall, it is a narrow path requiring sacrifice. So we must become one with the path so we can see and share it correctly, for in the end, the great spiritual path is everything.

Chapter Forty-Six

When we follow the great path, there is peace. When leaders follow the path, they realize that there is enough current suffering, and so they are not preparing for war. Often, conflict comes from greed, which is a bad trait to acquire; so be content with what you have and follow the great path.

Chapter Forty-Seven

As I said before, no prior special education or experience is needed to follow the great path to heaven. In fact, too much education and experience sometimes shows that less is known, and wise people learn this quickly. So keep an open mind to what the path can teach you.

Chapter Forty-Eight

Following the path requires gaining new knowledge, and this begins by letting go of much of the old knowledge you have and no longer need, which can take you off course. Yes, your old, preconceived thoughts and useless, prior education are distractions and must be left behind on the great journey you are about to undertake. However, when you do so, you can reach a pinnacle of self-actualization—a state of optimal self, as God intended—and you will have joyous inner peace. So don't manipulate the world for your own personal gain, for as the old adage goes, "You can gain the whole world and still lose your soul." Your life is not in this world but should be focused on the great path that leads to heaven.

Chapter Forty-Nine

Along the way, be kind and have no grudges, because most everyone is trying to do their best in their own eyes. So quickly forgive and have compassion for others. Don't expect too much from people and you won't be disappointed. Remember, God loves unconditionally, so you should do the same.

Chapter Fifty

Many people waste their lives pursuing activities that take them off course or reach for the pleasures of life that leave them unfulfilled. So live your life with great passion, but use cautious intelligence in those things you choose to do so you can stay on the great path.

Chapter Fifty-One

The great path has numerous tools for the person who follows it. When someone encounters the secrets of the right path, it can help raise them up, punish them, guide them, protect them, and it gives meaning and quality to life. More amazingly, it shows how valuable it is by accomplishing its goals without coercion or force. So follow the great path; its discipline will lead you to heaven.

Chapter Fifty-Two

Stay close to the great path until you die, for out of this journey springs forth the fruit of true growth. Of course, always take the time to notice the small things in life that make it so special, but don't get involved in the mundane things of an earthly life that take you off course. In the end, you need to keep your focus on the path and use the yin-yang flexibility it presents; for to be successful, you need to be "gentle as a dove and wary as a serpent."

Chapter Fifty-Three

The wrong path involves excessive time with wine, women, and song. Those who indulge in such things only care about themselves and are distracted from their focus. The right path avoids shortcuts, involves sacrifice, and requires a dedication to true wisdom.

Chapter Fifty-Four

The great path has been around forever and passed down from generation to generation. In fact, the path has been worshipped for its value, and if you don't let it slip from your grip, it will carry you to heaven. So take the great path within your spirit and pass it to your family, to the country, and to the world.

Chapter Fifty-Five

The grip of the great path gives harmony and lasting power, for those who have morals and character and who practice fairness are without condemnation or personal attack. And because the people practice self-control, the great path nourishes and illuminates life so its followers grow. So avoid the wrong path that leads to death, and take the true path that is blossoming, growing, and leads to life.

Chapter Fifty-Six

The words released from the tongue are important. In fact, each person is responsible for every idle word they speak, so speak from a heart of kindness rather than anger. Always try to speak of peace whenever possible, or be silent—for when you are silent, you benefit from non-action, and you eliminate unnecessary strife and anger. Even if you are right and the other person doesn't know what he is saying, harmful feelings may appear, and it simply isn't worth it trying to prove someone wrong. To sum up, if you let oneness and unity guide you in these endeavors, the world will stand up and take notice.

Chapter Fifty-Seven

What kind of leader do we need? Begin with fairness, which wins the trust of the people, as does respecting those who oppose you. Eliminate worry by not trying to overregulate the world. Anger and rebellion comes from too many laws (and the poor interpretation of those laws), too many guns, increasing fear, and a rise in cleverness and deception. So if a ruler can lead with wanting to truly help his people in his heart, and doesn't force his way with unnecessary demands, the people will respond with respect for this same leader, and they will make better choices for their families.

Chapter Fifty-Eight

The wise leader is able to get things done, and does so without constantly criticizing, micromanaging, or other forms of fault-finding—which often happen because of greed, ruining the chance of goodwill among the people. Instead, be like the wise leader who can accomplish much by correcting in a gentle way that lets people relax and focus on the task at hand.

Chapter Fifty-Nine

If you want to be an effective and welcomed leader and build confidence in your followers, you must first build the roots of the great path into the people. You must also win their trust and get them to believe in you, which happens when you use good judgment and are careful with the resources at hand. If you can do this, you can overcome anything as a ruler.

Chapter Sixty

The wise leader always rules the people with the wisdom of the great path in his mind, guiding his decisions. When leadership comes out of this sense of goodness, evil will be lessened, rebuked, and will not harm.

Chapter Sixty-One

People who want to work together will prosper. So think of others before yourself, join together, help each other, and be servants to each other so you can enjoy the benefits the great path has to offer.

Chapter Sixty-Two

Be certain, great kings and great riches cannot help you like the wisdom that is found in the great path. The worth of its wisdom has been known forever, and it becomes even more powerful because true followers cling to it without desire for their own wants. If a person's deeds and words along the journey are wise, great peace can and will be found. In the end, this oneness with the path eventually leads to the wonderful joys waiting in heaven.

Chapter Sixty-Three

Situations and problems will arise that will require your attention. When this happens, do not delay; treat every circumstance as an emergency that needs to be dealt with quickly. When you act early, you can correct a potential problem before it gets too big. When you eliminate problems while they are small, it means you will be more successful in life. So make an honest evaluation of what is going on, get involved, and don't be discouraged; for even in the worst situation, you can respond to evil with good.

Chapter Sixty-Four

Some things in life should be obvious, like in the case of handling projects. The best way to get things done in life is to start early before you dig a hole for yourself. Therefore, the best way to accomplish a goal is to act on it early without delay, otherwise you will have to rush to finish the project. Why does this happen? It is usually because of a lack of planning, which often leads to failure. So if you want to be successful, be as careful and thorough in the beginning as you are at the end. This is how a great leader helps people; he plans, puts his desires aside, learns the heart of his followers, and helps them with genuine concern, rather than acting like a ruler over them.

Chapter Sixty-Five

While you are on the great path, character and credibility are important. Two key factors here are always being honest, and having a clear message that you are trying to convey. If you use deceit or cheat people, these lies will catch up to you. Remember that people will follow others who have integrity, even though some are misled by thinking that telling others what they want to hear sounds better when it actually is deception. So make your message clear, honest, and simple.

Chapter Sixty-Six

What kind of leader do you want to be? Well, consider the volume of the seas; this equates to the volume of support you will receive from followers if you speak from a true heart of humbleness and don't set up walls of oppression for them. If these things happen, not only will the people accept you, they will clamor for your leadership.

Chapter Sixty-Seven

If we listen to the wisdom of the great path, it tells us how to live. For example, it begins by advising us to have no desire for ourselves, but instead, by having great compassion and love for others. Next, be considerate of others, and don't think of yourself as better than anyone else. In fact, have empathy for others, and have something to give to them. Learn at your own pace, and share your thoughts, but don't brag about your superiority or brilliance. Remember, life is not worth living without being able to share love and compassion. If we rely on heaven along the way, our compassion will be rewarded with compassion.

Chapter Sixty-Eight

Sometimes along the journey, you will be put on the defensive, so you will need methods to guard your position. First, approach any situation with balance and composure. Next, keep your wits about you, and take no foolish risks. Remember, the best defense is an approach where attack or war is not needed. As a counterattack, treat people with respect and better than you treat yourself. There is great reward in defusing a person's anger, appealing to their talent, or catching them doing something you can praise them about. If you can do this, the heavens will rejoice.

Chapter Sixty-Nine

If you have opponents in life, weigh the options and resources you have on hand. Next, determine whether you need to give ground in a conflict, or debate and stand your ground. In other words, you must "know when to hold 'em, know when to fold 'em." Then keep your real weapons hidden, and instead, try to use the surprise attack of trying to settle a conflict without a fight. In the end, keep a proper respect for opponents, and don't take anyone for granted; for if you do, it could mean defeat.

Chapter Seventy

The laws of wisdom come from the experience earned while following the great path. Yet many people do not understand this journey or practice what is taught on the wise road. In fact, if all people were able to understand me, I would not be needed. However, those that are lost blindly follow their own desires. Because of this, my teaching is valuable.

Chapter Seventy-One

When walking on the great path, there are certain ways to earn respect. First, admit the things you do wrong. Next, admit that you don't know everything. These two things will help you relate to other people that you are human and have much to learn. Not admitting that you are sometimes wrong or thinking you know everything is both arrogance and illness.

Chapter Seventy-Two

Along the path, there are standing rules for leading people. First, let go of your desire to control others. Next, lead without coercion or force. Finally, don't get into people's personal business or use it against them to keep them down. When you accomplish these things, not only will you respect yourself, you will win the people over.

Chapter Seventy-Three

Heaven has a vast array of resources to offer along the great path, but there is a right way to do things. This is not always easy, as even leaders sometimes can't understand heaven and its ways. So first, learn to relax and limit any worrying. Next, set the goals that the path requires. After this, reach out and gather information, and listen to others. Finally, it comes down to choices. For instance, if you have the choice between being brave and foolish, or just being brave, pick just being brave without taking silly risks. When you combine courage and intelligence, you come out on top.

Chapter Seventy-Four

If you want to be a great leader, treat people fairly, and don't make idle threats against them. If you constantly instill fear in your followers, people will come to hate you and revolt. Be aware, others may take this wrong road, but if you follow this unwise path, you will only harm yourself.

Chapter Seventy-Five

One of the greatest virtues a leader can have is the propensity to ponder the needs of the people he rules over; for when he treats his people from a place of compassion, he can live in peace and prosperity. This is the opposite of a greedy ruler who demands higher taxes and angers those under his rule. If a ruler stirs up these negative emotions, the followers will not fear him and revolt.

Chapter Seventy-Six

There are two ways to live your life. Unfortunately, for adults on the wrong path, life can be hard, so they become unwavering, cynical, harsh, cold, bitter, and critical. Now think of how a child first approaches the world. A child is open-minded, full of acceptance for the world around him, soft with compassion, and gentle when encountering others. In the end, he is hoping to give and receive love. Be like the child, for this is the right path to take.

Chapter Seventy-Seven

How should we help people? Well, let's first start with the wrong way to do it. This non-path would include becoming more and more greedy, stealing from the poor, pretending to help, or not helping at all. The right path is simple; those that can help others should do so without bragging and in a totally unselfish way. In the end, the road to heaven involves giving to others in need.

Chapter Seventy-Eight

If you accept corruption in your life, it will become your master, so you must come up with a plan to handle all situations that arise. For instance, take a clue from water, which is persistent with success because it adapts to its surroundings. This is different than the inflexible rock, which can be worn down by water. Though appearing soft and gentle, water is persistent in getting the results it seeks. So to be successful, remember this: stay on the great path, focus on the goal, and be like water.

Chapter Seventy-Nine

Let me remind you: don't get angry and start interfering into other people's business, for if you do this, these same people will hold a grudge against you and not forget. Also, become a person of integrity by keeping the promises you make, for broken promises mean a lack of integrity. Always remember that credibility is important on the great path.

Chapter Eighty

Remember what is important in life. Always value life and enjoy it. Keep your life as simple as possible, for this is a precious path. Next, protect yourself when you have to, and stay out of quarrels as much as possible. Finally, truly give people what they need in terms of food, clothes, shelter, and compassion, for this promotes peace with our neighbors.

Chapter Eighty-One

We must learn the path by experiencing it, for even educated people are foolish in their understanding of life. So keep focused on the simplicity of the path instead of the complexity of examination. In fact, those without formal education that faithfully follow the path understand all. Also, be simple in speech so you can avoid arguments and be at peace. Next, always remember that we have a loving God—not a selfish God—who wants to put us on the right path, for heaven is here to help us, not harm us. Finally, in the end, follow the path set forth here, for it is the great way.

About the Author

Kevin M. Thomas is an award-winning author of titles like, *Tao Te Ching De-Coded* and *Why Daughters Need Their Dads*, and has a varied background in medicine, alternative health, counseling, religion, and mind-body healing. Kevin is passionate about promoting and delivering positive change to any person, and he strives to affect personal growth in individuals via mind-body-spirit research and application. Finally, he considers his relationship with God and his unconditional love for his children—Isiah, Caroline, Kimberly, and Cheyenne—as his greatest treasures.

Wisdom and Virtue

Wisdom and Virtue is a decoded and paraphrased version of the *Tao Te Ching*, which dates back to 600BCE. This book takes the eighty-one chapters that help make up Taoism, Chinese Philosophy, and Chinese Religion and simplifies them for easy, everyday application and use. Growing in popularity over the years, the *Tao Te Ching* is the second-most translated book in the world behind the Bible, and the passages contained within can contribute to real personal growth on a mental, spiritual, and even physical level.

KETNA PUBLISHING: Kevin Thomas and Erik Naugle make up KETNA Publishing, a small, hometown publisher located in mid-Michigan. Their goal is to deliver high-quality information into the hands of the people so they can positively change their lives via body, mind, and spirit application. You can contact KETNA Publishing at kt123trailblazer@gmail.com or grobthom@aol.com or write to KETNA Publishing, P.O. Box 90861, Burton, Michigan, 48509.

www.ingramcontent.com/pod-product-compliance
Lightning Source LLC
Chambersburg PA
CBHW070546300426
44113CB00011B/1804